HELP!
My Guru Died

HELP!
My Guru Died

Questions and Answers to make your old-time religion right on, your sects sexier, your cults more culpable.

By SWAMI RAMI SALAMI

Translated from Sanskrit By Harry Krishna

Etchings by Erocs Spordnoom

 POP BOOKS

RANDOM HOUSE

A PREFACE BY
THE GREAT, GREAT ONE

When sorrow comes, you must rise above it—
as the beautiful waves rise soft, gently,
inscrutably over the thick, heavy, ugly clunk
of a rock.

When joy comes, you must seize it—as the rolling
ocean reaches out a warm, comforting hand
and catches the afternoon sunset. If you don't,
some damn fool will run off with your joy.
I remember once in Omaha . . .

Love is akin to hate, as entrails are akin to skin.

War is a brother to peace—just as *Brother, Can
You Spare a Dime* was a popular song. Other
popular songs I like are *Get A Job, Work With
Me, Annie,* and *Oh, My Papa.*

Ah . . . but enough of my wisdom for now. More
will be revealed in these pages.

Yours in peace and wisdom and whatever,

The Great, Great One
(From his hilltop)

Q: The minister of our church has absconded with the money given by the faithful — and one of the faithful (female) as well. Do you think this man is a real servant of the Lord?

A: Judge not. The servant problem grows worse day by day.

§ § §

Q: I am beset by hardships. Tasks, plants, animals, forests, persons, storms, allurements, repulsions, houses, books, machines, fire, water, earth, and an intricate humanity.

A: Thank God, at least you're normal — now what's your problem?

Q: My husband comes home every night — well, *almost* every night, tanked to the gills. Should I divorce him?

A: Personally I think there's something fishy about your husband.

§ § §

Q: My doctor says I should have 1/3 of my stomach removed or I will die. My faith does not allow surgery. What should I do?

A: Nothing. Time and your faith will take care of everything.

§ § §

Q: I am a young man and I seem to like boys better than girls.

A: Oh…have I got a boy for you.

Q: My best friend threw acid at me and the whole left side of my face is sort of gone. And my friend's girl won't look at me any more.

A: If you turn the other cheek, you're crazy.

§ § §

Q: We have been married for 13 years and haven't anything to say to each other any more.

A: I have nothing to say to this.

§ § §

Q: I work in a mine 6 1/2 days a week and get to sit down on Sunday afternoons. Should I do the sitting in church, or do what I want to do — stay home and soak my feet?

A: For the best of all possible worlds, take a bucket of water to church… or a Bible to the bathtub.

Q: I would like to see things with clarity, but even more, to feel them keenly.

A: Stay away from Andy Warhol movies.

§ § §

Q: Eleven years ago I robbed a bank and still have plenty of money left, but somehow my conscience is beginning to bother me.

A: Send me the money at once and depending on what's left, I'll do what I can.

Q: My mother shows Lesbian tendencies.

A: Everybody has to be someplace.

Q: In a street riot last month, I threw a Molotov cocktail that hit an old lady. Should I turn myself in?

A: Yes, into a human torch.

§ § §

Q: My brother keeps putting his hand around my waist, you know, in a funny place. P.S. I am a girl.

A: Either your brother has a large hand or you have a small waist.

Q: I have 13 children and none of them send me a Christmas card.

A: Are you Jewish?

§ § §

Q: I have a neighbor who sneaks out at night after her husband is asleep. Should I tell him about this?

A: Not while you're making love.

§ § §

Q: I have worked in the same job for 17 years and have never had a raise.

A: Tell your boss, "The Gander could use a Goose."

Q: I try to run my house, raise my children, and give my husband his beer and liverwurst. I also work 55 hours a week. Is it right that I feel tired?

A: Camellias have died whilst we kneel by rosebuds to pray their bloom. (I don't know what the hell that means, but I thought I'd throw it in.)

Q: I have engaged in lots and lots of perversion. Should I look for help?

A: Apparently you've gotten it.

§ § §

Q: My house burned down, I lost my job, my wife was run over, my kid is in jail. How can I go on?

A: The insurance should help.

§ § §

Q: I have varicose veins, eczema, chronic halitosis, hemorrhoids, asthma and, at the moment of writing, a common cold. What's a body to do?

A: Apparently, yours will wither and die.

Q: I have this thing for furs and diamonds. (I am 24 and rather beautiful.) Don't you think it's all right for me to crave these things?

A: Right on, baby?

Q: I don't believe I've ever had a prayer answered. Is anybody really listening?

A: He listened, until you started getting pushy.

§ § §

Q: I can't afford anything better than my room near Times Square. The din is driving me bananas.

A: It's pronounced den, not din.

Q: I have lost the God-spark. Can I ever find it again?

A: Take a sprig of parsley, two of sage, three of rosemary and four of thyme, boil 20 minutes. It ain't soul food, baby, but any potion is better than no potion.

Q: I think I must be the original fall guy. It rains every time I play golf, elevators get stuck when I'm in them, I blow my nose on cocktail napkins, and always get in the slow line at the bank. Will this nonsense ever stop?

A: Probably not.

§ § §

Q: In school I have to write a paper on Moby Dick and I can't make any sense out of the silly book.

A: Well…it's about this whale…

Q: My sister has gone from pot to hash to acid to opium. I am frantic.

A: Your religion has no doubt kept you in good stead. Try getting her some FRANTIC tracts.

§ § §

Q: Can you tell me why I have this mad thing for rutabagas? I can't seem to get enough.

A: Very, very kinky.

Q: The kneeling benches in our church are full of splinters. So are my panty-hose.

A: Stand up for Jesus.

Q: I love this man, see, but he only seems attracted to me when we are in bed. Is something wrong?

A: Yes. Help him get on his feet.

Q: I am a young man and I seem to like boys better than girls.

A: Everybody's gotta be someplace.

§ § §

Q: I quit the jet set, gave all my money to a shelter for unwanted pets. Now I live in a rooming house, am often hungry, and am beginning to wonder if I made a mistake.

A: Console yourself with Alpo.

§ § §

Q: I have acne. It's confined to my nose.

A: Have you had your nose in somebody else's business?

Q: Our daughter ran away with the town stud after she forged a check and emptied my bank account. What can I do?

A: Be happy for her.

Q: I marched in a Women's Lib parade and my boy friend hasn't spoken to me since.

A: Forget it. You'll soon have three girl friends for every boy who's turned you down.

§ § §

Q: Hare Krishna?

A: Same to you.

§ § §

Q: What can I do with my sister?

A: With relaxation of state and national moral laws, almost anything.

Q: My husband snores something awful. It's like drums and train whistles and people choking to death. How do I get a decent night's sleep?

A: Join a band, take a trip, kill somebody…and thereby relate.

§ § §

Q: I get A's in math and science but I keep flunking art and literature.

A: It is possible that you are not intellectual, not effete, and not a snob.

Q: I have had a migraine headache for a year and five months.

A: Perhaps you are not well.

Q: My ambition is to paint the ceiling of our den just like Michelangelo's Sistine Chapel. Is this sacrilegious?

A: Is the Pope Catholic?

§ § §

Q: I love my girl friend, but I keep getting this urge to stab her foot with my Boy Scout penknife.

A: See? Just like the Scoutmaster said, that knife would come in handy one day.

§ § §

Q: I think my great-aunt is a lush. I keep finding half empty bottles in the oddest places.

A: Don't look in the oddest places.

Q: Can you believe a wife who refuses to darn her husband's socks?

A: Sure.

Q: All my friends relate to rock festivals but I don't dig these things. What's wrong with me?

A: Even though they're heavier, try throwing bricks.

§ § §

Q: I am all alone in this world. I have only the photographs of my dead family.

A: I use a Nikon with a wide-angle lens and, of course, always a filter on cloudy days.

Q: My mother hates me, my father hates me, my sister hates me.

A: Perhaps deep down inside, where it truly counts, you are really detestable.

Q: What about that original sin business? Am I to go through life all bent over because of what Adam and Eve did one dumb day?

A: If you're bent, don't blame Adam and Eve — the Bible tells us they were straight.

§ § §

Q: My husband beats me every Monday, Wednesday and Friday with a billy club he stole from a London bobby. I am a bloody mess. How can I continue to love this beast I married?

A: Call Masochists Anonymous.

Q: To tell you the truth, I don't understand a damned thing any more. What is wrong with me?

A: Perhaps your name is Agnew.

§ § §

Q: After eight tragic love affairs, I think I have finally found Mr. Right. How can I be sure?

A: Do something wrong to test his reaction.

Q: My wife of 46 years is having an affair with the man next door.

A: Catered or casual?

§ § §

Q: How many hours a day should I pray?

A: How many hours have you got?

§ § §

Q: I get indigestion from meat, vegetables, fish, poultry, fruit, dairy products and all desserts. I feel faint.

A: Stop feeling faint—in public. Anyway, after all, he's got feelings too.

Q: My kid is impossible. He fights with every kid on the block, steals everything he can lay his hands on, and yesterday he kicked his grandmother in the shins.

A: Stop writing me these crank notes!

§ § §

Q: My stockbroker, who moonlights as a parson, tells me it's God's will I should hang on to a stock that has gone from 176 to 3¼.

A: Is your stock in temples or churches?

Q: My wife's family is terrible. Her father is a drunk, her mother's a hop head, her brother is an unemployed bum. Can you give me a thought to help me bear these relatives?

A: Always remember, everything in life is relative.

§ § §

Q: I have been in public school for 17 years — three years in the 12th grade already. And I'm sick and tired of it.

A: You spell well.

Q: I am 18 and my parents still chain me to the bedstead.

A: Everyone has to be someplace.

Q: My son, a brilliant, handsome and wonderful boy of 46, has been going with a really terrible girl for 14 years. I am desperately afraid he will have to marry her.

A: He probably shares your feelings.

§ § §

Q: Should I meditate in the morning or evening?

A: It is good to ask such a question.

Q: I was adopted and my mother says I was found in some bullrushes. Isn't this a bit unusual?

A: Not if your father was a bull.

§ § §

Q: I am an admitted alcoholic, and every time I take Communion, the wine sends me off on a binge. Should I quit going to church, or what?

A: What.

Q: My husband gave me a strange looking vibrator for Christmas. Is he putting me on?

A: No, he's attempting to plug you in.

§ § §

Q: I am a schoolteacher and can't control my classes. The kids have graduated from spitballs to bricks. What can I do about this?

A: Perhaps your local school board will bus you.

Q: I am trying to fight City Hall, and I find it an endless bureaucracy, staffed by pompous idiots.

A: May thy rod and thy staff comfort thee.

§ § §

Q: My boss is a married man, and I am guilty of loving him.

A: Join the club.

Q: I am sure my landlady keeps coming into my apartment while I'm at work.

A: Raise rats.*

§ § §

Q: My husband insists on eating dinner in his underwear. I am a Christian woman, but some things I can't put up with.

A: Bring something to your relationship and to your dinner table...if only a veil.

*Write for my free booklet, *Raising Rats For Fun and Profit.* Enclose $25.00 for mailing and handling charges.

Q: I am continually on a mountaintop. I feel I'm teetering, about to fall. My arms reach out to you. Help me!

A: If the mountain tumbles, so shall the climber.

§ § §

Q: Our teenage son's hair is so long that he had another hairy friend for dinner the other night, and we couldn't tell which one was our son. Jesus kept his hair out of his face—can't today's kids?

A: It is written, Jesus had disciples and a hairnet.

Q: How come I get such a kick out of church? I can't wait for Sundays.

A: Perhaps you are a Sabbath freak, or you have a groovy priest.

Q: I have ironed in this laundry since 1938 and last week they made this guy Head Ironer who only started working here last month. I am so mad I could spit on my iron (which I never do).

A: I realize you had seniority, but the boss liked the color of his eyes.

§ § §

Q: I am a girl 5′ 11″, and I am fantastically in love with a boy who is 5′ 3″.

A: Buy him a pair of Bermuda shorts — it's time he wore long pants.

Q: I work at Macy's (pots and pans) and watch TV at night because my feet hurt. My friends say I don't think enough.

A: How about spreading around some of that pot?

§ § §

Q: I have had a heart condition for 78 years and never had a word of sympathy from my son.

A: Leave your money to science, and your diseased heart to your son.

Q: I bathe every day and use Ban, but nobody loves me.

A: Some people just don't dig Ban.

Q: I am a volunteer in the Peace Corps. The country where I work had a revolution last week, and I was raped by 174 men within a 20-hour period. How can I go on?

A: Have you considered changing your vocation?

§ § §

Q: My wife and her best friend are acting very suspicious lately. I think they are lovers. What can I do?

A: If they won't consider a threesome, ask if you can watch.

Q: I no longer burn purely.

A: Perhaps you're using the wrong kind of matches.

§ § §

Q: Every time I go to the pool hall I find myself attracted to the guy who runs the place. Frankly, I'm worried.

A: Join the queue.

Q: I can't relate to my mother-in-law.

A: Attempt a relationship with your father-in-law.

Q: What do I do after evensong?

A: What an odd question to ask.